It's the

Little

Things

That can change your life!

By

Tage N. Wright

Acknowledgements:

I would like to acknowledge my wife of over forty years for the support she has given me in all of my endeavors. I would also like to thank Louise Kahler for her tireless effort in editing this book as well as the others I have written. I would also like to thank my granddaughter Samantha Swift for the drawings on the front cover and my daughter Viola for the cover design.

Dedication:

I would like to dedicate this work to the memory of my Mother and Father, Fred and Sophie Wright, who made my life possible. There is a peace given to me in the sure and certain knowledge that they are together once again.

Chapter 1
"Who is your Hero?"

How do you define a hero? The dictionary defines a hero as a man of distinguished courage or ability, admired for his brave deeds and noble qualities. Sometimes the dictionary just doesn't quite get it done. Perhaps as we move along you will see what mean.

A few years ago, during a performance of "Legends in Concert" at Foxwoods Casino in Montville, Connecticut the guy doing the Elvis impersonation had the lights turned up in the auditorium. He asked all of the military veterans to stand, then the policemen and then the firemen. He told the rest of the audience to look at those standing because they were the real heroes.

Gosh, it felt really good to stand there knowing that someone actually appreciated the four years I spent in the Navy and the seven years in the Army National Guard. The funny part about this is that most of us who serve our country don't think of ourselves as heroes not even those who do heroic deeds. If you asked Audie Murphy if he was a hero what do you think he would have said? Do you even know who he was?

I was in McDonalds some time ago and I asked the young man behind the counter if he knew who Audie Murphy was, he didn't. I then asked him if he knew who Alvin York was, he didn't know that either. When I asked him who Sponge Bob was he pointed to the picture of our yellow friend on the wall behind me.

At least I know who is famous at the McDonalds in Gales Ferry.

If you don't know who the other two guys were I'll fill you in. They were Medal of Honor recipients and two of the most highly decorated combat soldiers in our nation's history. I don't know how much we spend on public education but I am sure it is more than enough so that we might learn who our national heroes are and what they did.

You know that fifteen minutes of fame thing people talk about? It was originally coined by Andy Warhol in 1968. Well I think that it might just go for being a hero too. We all get to be a hero if we so choose. Just like we all get to be famous for those fifteen minutes.

I've already had my fifteen minutes. There is a plaque in my living room that was given to me by the Post Office for saving a mailman from a couple of Pit Bulls that were trying to eat him. It says "for your heroic actions" in chasing the dogs away. At the time I didn't think it was heroic, I just thought it was a good idea seeing that the dogs were doing their best to kill the poor guy. Since I am not afraid of dogs and I had a framing hammer in my hand I didn't think twice. I just went after the dogs. If they decided to eat me as well I would have simply killed them both. I knew that in the end they would both be put down anyway.

My point here is that most "heroes" don't start out figuring that they are going to be a hero. They usually do what they think is the right thing to do at the time.

A common thread in all of this is an individual's lack of hesitation to sacrifice, whether it be their treasure or even their life, for the sake of someone else. They don't expect fame or fortune. They just want to do the right thing.

There is a song by Harry Chapin that says a little about this subject. It's called "The Rock" and it's the story of a hero. It is just a song but in song we often find the truth that we don't see even if it is right in front of us. The hero of this song sacrifices his own life to save a town full of people who think he is daft.

The song highlights another quality of a hero- they don't concern themselves what others might think. They do what they know is the right thing to do and don't take opinion polls before doing it. When a mother sacrifices her own wants and even needs to take care of her children some think that is foolish. Yet there is no hero greater than a mother in the eyes of her children. My wife has graduated to an elevated hero status, she is a hero to our grandchildren and she deserves the title.

When I think of a hero, I also think of my father who armed with a few hand tools and a pencil built a house for us to live in. I think of my mother who took care of us when we were sick. When I was a teenager looking for work she helped me get my first part-time job. I think of my wife who would charge into any situation regardless of the danger to protect her family. Heroes don't all carry guns or fight in wars, although there are plenty of those types of heroes to go around.

There isn't a special school for heroes or a government program to make you into one. It is strictly on-the-job training. You can improve your chances of becoming a hero though. The best way to do that is to make some changes which increase the possibility of being a hero.

You know, try to develop some of the traits you see common in hero types. It's easier than trying to pass the test to become a fireman or a police officer.

Wait a minute! I see a problem here already. The whole deal would revolve around who you see as a hero! This is more complicated than I originally thought it would be. What if your hero is really a villain? I'm going to have to take a leap of faith here and assume that your idea of a hero is not going to turn out to be a villain.

Courage is one characteristic of a hero. But what is courage? It is the ability to face one's fears with calm resolution. That is a mouthful and it isn't the half of it. I'll bet you have all kinds of courage hiding out inside of you just waiting to show itself. What did the Wizard of Oz give the lion who thought he was a coward? I can tell you what he said to the lion.

"As for you my fine friend, you are a victim of disorganized thinking. You are under the unfortunate delusion that simply because you run away from danger you have no courage. You are confusing courage with wisdom."

You should be aware of this simple fact; courage is not the absence of fear. Fear is a good thing. It is your personal danger detector. Fear is why a deer runs from a mountain lion. Without it he would be dinner.

Panic on the other hand is not good. That is when your fear overpowers your courage. Panic can get you killed.

If you want to be a hero start at home and work up from there. Not many of us will be in a situation where we can demonstrate to the world our heroic qualities. You know what, that doesn't amount to a hill of beans (I've always wondered what that saying meant!). I can prove it. I've been asking people who their heroes are. They weren't who you would expect. In many cases it was a parent! That should tell you something!!

In the end most of us don't look to the heroes society picks to be our special heroes. In the end we want our heroes to be much closer to home. We want heroes who touch us in a way that an Audie Murphy or Alvin York can't.

If you want to be a hero you can start by learning how to serve those around you. Who better to start with than your own family? You want instant hero status? Try your children first.

Some of us might not have children to be heroes to. You are not off of the hook! Just look around you. My Daughter the school bus driver is a hero to most of the kids on her bus especially to her niece (my granddaughter) who rides that bus. So forge ahead and become a hero. It's easier than you think!

Remember, you don't have to be Superman to be a hero. In fact, you don't even have to be a man!!

Chapter 2
"Dreams"

Do you remember your dreams? I don't mean the dreams you have when you're asleep; I mean the ones you have when you are awake. The ones you think about when you are not on life's merry go round. Do you remember those dreams?

When we are kids we dream all the time. Back when I was in first grade in that little two room schoolhouse in Center Groton I would dream about what I wanted to be when I got big. I drew pictures of airplanes on the back of my schoolwork because I wanted to be a pilot.

I always remembered wanting to fly planes but I had forgotten about drawing the pictures until about twenty years later when my motorcycle broke down on North Road. There weren't any cell phones back then so I went to the nearest house and knocked on the door.

To my surprise one of my teachers from that little schoolhouse came to the door. She let me use her phone to call for help and we sat and talked for a while. She said she always remembered how I drew pictures on the back of my schoolwork.

I was glad she didn't remember me from the time I jumped out the cloak room window and wound up staying after school with my head down on the desk. They knew how to teach you a lesson back then. Absolutely nothing matched being put in the older kids' classroom with your head down on the desk.

When I think of dreams I think of the song "Dreams Go By" written and performed by Harry Chapin. Here he is again, good old Harry. I don't know if you know who he was, but if you don't you have missed some great music. That song puts what happens to most of our dreams in perspective. It begins like this….

There you stand in your dungarees, looking so grown up and so very pleased. When you write your poems they have so much to say. When you speak your dreams it takes my breath away. You know I want to be a ball player, a regular slugging fool. But I guess our dreams must wait awhile. Until we finish school.

Isn't that how our dreams seem to go? There is usually something else that takes their spot. Well, I guess if you think about it, when someone calls you a daydreamer, or even just a dreamer it isn't usually meant as a compliment and in some ways being "practical" means ignoring your dreams. And guess what happens…

*And so you and I
We watch our years go by
We watch our sweet dreams fly
Far away, but maybe someday*

Yup, maybe someday, I've heard that tune more than once in my life. In fact I've been guilty of singing it once or twice or, never mind how many times. How about you? Do you have a dream you keep hidden away for just the right time? It just lies there waiting for the right time to jump up and say; "Hello it's me your dream come and get me!"

And so the song goes,

I don't know when
But we will dream again
And we'll be happy then
Till our time just drifts away

Once you let your dream slip away another might just sneak up on you. It's not over yet!! Hey, when you get older your likes and dislikes change. You develop a new talent and bingo you have another dream. I let my dream of flying through the air slip away. In High School I learned you could fly along on the ground, I got my license to drive!

That's when my love affair with the motorcar began. I really liked sports cars and I owned several back then. It started back in High School when I bought a 1963 TR-4. I loved that car. It had a little four-cylinder motor that pushed the car to 107 miles per hour. That's when I began to dream about racing. Yup, another dream came along and replaced the old one.

Has that happened to you? Sure it has. What did you do? I'll tell you what I did, I put my dream on hold while I visited my Uncle Sam and helped him out in a place called Viet Nam. When I got back from that, another little thing came up that, well, sort of canceled the racecar thing.

> *There you stand in your wedding dress*
> *You're so beautiful that I must confess*
> *I'm so proud you have chosen me*
> *When a doctor is what you want to be*
>
> *You know I want to be a painter, girl*
> *A real artistic snob*
> *But I guess we'll have our children first*
> *You'll find a home I'll get a job*

You guessed it I got married. You probably have the gist of the whole dream deal by now. Dreams are what make us human. I doubt that a Poodle dreams of being Saint Bernard, although I knew a Poodle who thought he was a Doberman. I certainly doubt that a horse dreams of being the winner at Belmont. And I really don't believe that Charlie the Tuna dreamt of ending up in a can of StarKist.

Listen it's our dreams that make us special. It's when we pursue our dreams that we are building the world we want to live in. When someone calls you a "dreamer" thank that individual for the compliment, because whether they mean it that way or not, it is one of the highest compliment you can get.

Are you willing to chase after your dream? It can be a hard battle. Even when you have obtained that dream the struggle may not be over. Sometimes when you think you have a dream firmly in your grasp someone comes along and tries to rip it away. And sometimes they win….

Take the case of Susette Kelo. I know about her dream because of a book. Hey, I write books. But I write fiction. I make them up from start to finish. The people in my books have the dreams that I gave them. At least that's how I think it works. Sometimes I wonder….

Enough of that, back to Susette, you will find her story in a book called "Little Pink House" by Jeff Benedict, someone I've known since he was a teenager. Jeff has skills when it comes to getting to the root of a story.

Under the title on the cover of the book is the subtitle "A True Story of Defiance and Courage". In addition to that, this story is about the willingness for someone to fight against seemingly insurmountable odds to keep her dream, the "Little Pink House".

If you have ever had a dream you gave up because the fight got the best of you, you need to read this book. I know it makes my dream battles seem rather small and makes me think I gave up too soon on more than one occasion. Please visit Jeff's website, Jeffbendict.com and learn more about what it means to fight for a dream.

If you don't seek after your dreams you will be singing right along with good old Harry Chapin…..

There you stand in your tailored suit
So many years gone by but you're still so cute

You take the car to go and meet the bus
When our grandchildren come to visit us

You say you should have been a ballerina, babe
There are songs I should have sung
But I guess our dreams have come and gone
You've gotta dream when you are young

If you have a dream that you can wrap yourself around, go get it. Just one word of advice though, if your dream is to get a job as a Ninja (like my son's when he was ten) it might be a hard sell.

Just keep dreaming and if you are married to a dreamer fasten your seat belt because you are in for the ride of your life!

I saw a tee shirt yesterday that had a sign on it. It said, "some people follow their dreams while some hunt them down". Perhaps you should hunt down that dream of yours and make it happen.

If you have a dream worth having, then it's worth fighting for. So, get suited up and get to work and don't stop until it becomes more than just a dream.

Chapter 3
"You Can't fix Stupid"

A long time ago when I was working for Dow Biopharmaceuticals a coworker, Pam Bennit, told me that you couldn't fix stupid. Being a fix it kind of guy I wasn't sure I agreed with her analysis, only lately I'm leaning more toward her being correct at least a good part of the time.

I suppose that since we just passed through the political season the concept of "Stupidity" is more obvious than usual. As if it wasn't already too prevalent! I looked up stupid to see if my understanding of the word actually coincides with reality. I especially liked the comment in one of the definitions that "stupid" is in the eye of the beholder. That gives us all some room to be stupid.

I have come to the conclusion that no matter how smart you are you can still be stupid. Take the gal who designed the toilets used in the Westerly Rhode Island Hospital. I'm sure that she is quite smart. I say gal because a guy would have realized that the distance from where your bottom rests to the water level would be insufficient for the male anatomy and that is all the detail I want to add to that subject!

I refrained from writing my blog during the crazy time running up to the last election because I have some very strong opinions and I didn't want to drive away readers with my political views. I like to write about things that just might help the reader have a happier life no matter which side of the isle you sit on.

There are some times when you do need to hold your tongue. Then there are other time when holding your tongue only gets you a sore tongue. I don't need a sore tongue this week.

There are however some things that you just have to comment on and let whatever is going to happen, happen because after the horrific event in Newtown, Connecticut for me being stupid took on a very different face.

When your stupidity results in part of your body getting wet when you sit on a toilet there is nothing lost, but when being stupid has the end result of someone losing their life it is a whole different matter. I will get into that a bit later, for now here is some of the less tragic stupidity out there.

In September of last year New York City banned soft drinks of larger than 16 oz. at restaurants, mobile food carts, sports arenas and movie theaters. Presumably you can still buy two 16 oz. drinks only you won't have a free hand to hold the candy bar that they will probably ban next. If that isn't stupid enough the gal who wrote the article that I read called it a "bold experiment in the anti-obesity campaign". It gets even better.

She claimed that it is widely supported by health professionals. I don't know who those professionals are but their middle name is Stupid. (Note the use of a capital S) If they think that limiting the size of the drink is going to accomplish anything other than costing the guy or gal who will now buy two drinks instead of one, more money they are, well, Stupid. As always, the winner here is the taxman and possibly the people who make the cups.

There is still good news in all of this. You can still buy alcoholic beverages in the larger size because they are exempt. Happy days are here again. Instead of being poisoned by that nasty sugar you can get smashed with a thirty two ounce glass of beer or wine or, hey this **is** stupid.

Wait just a minute, is having a beer belly considered obese? I guess since beer is exempt the beer belly must be okay. Maybe we should ask those health professionals about it. Nah, they are probably too busy figuring out what to ban from the school lunch programs.

Just a little side note on this obesity thing when I went to visit my doctor he told me that by the new standards that they have set I am now considered obese. I have no idea exactly who they are but *they* certainly seem to get around. The deal here is that I actually lost ten pounds from the last time I went to see him. That was when I wasn't obese. I'm confused. Someone is stupid here and I'm not sure just who it is.

Here is the problem and perhaps you would agree. People's weight is not something the government should be trying to control. The United States is supposed to be the land of the free. That is what I fought for when I put on the uniform (Army and Navy). If your snap answer is that it is a public health issue, I would remind you that the label "a public health issue" can apply to just about everything you do every day and the rule makers know that. Watch out you sun bathers; they are coming after you next. Ever hear of skin cancer?

When I googled stupid I discovered a list of thirty stupid things the government spends money on, how about this one, three million bucks to research video games. I wonder if I can get in on that. I play video games! I can do the research for half price, oh wait, I don't have a master's degree in doing studies, never mind. Here is another one, sixteen to twenty million to help Indonesians get masters degrees. I could use one of those. Then I could do the video game thing. Never mind, I can't afford to move to Indonesia. There are twenty-eight more, you should check them out.

You run into stupid just about everywhere you go. Many years ago when I owned a contracting business I went to a local hardware store to get something. I asked one of the owners if they gave contractor discounts. He said they didn't. Then came the stupid part, he asked, "Why would you want a discount?" I didn't have an answer for him. It was my turn to be stupid.

Now for the serious part of the discussion, since the horrible events in Newtown people in high places have been displaying stupidity at an alarming rate. What happened in that school is more than a tragedy. For me, the most terrible part is that had people who make the decisions done things differently perhaps most of it could have been prevented and I'll tell you why.

I recently watched a video of a ten minute standoff between an armed resource officer and an armed individual who was later shot dead by the police. That school resource officer protected the kids in that school and saved lives that would have otherwise been taken. Whoever it was who decided to have an armed individual in that school saved lives.

If I were responsible for keeping armed guards out of the Connecticut schools I would not be sleeping well right now or for that matter, ever again. To not have provided some kind of protection for the kids was Stupid and the kids paid the ultimate price for that stupidity.

So here is just a note to all those who make the decisions about such matters, if you oppose armed guards of some type in our schools and you are successful in keeping them out remember this; if another event like Newtown takes place you will have to live with that. In addition, I hope you never get a decent night's sleep again here or in the place you go to when you leave this earth.

When I was in the Navy I was a security guard for the missile house and I had to qualify each year with the model 1911 Colt .45 that I carried. I hit what I shoot at and I have no doubt at all that had I (or someone like myself) been in the office at Newtown with my sidearm that lunatic would not have gotten past the front entrance.

There was another article written by an Alma Rutgers stating that if we do put armed guards in schools the "Newtown gunman wins and the children lose". What? I have no idea who Alma Rutgers is but here is a news flash for her, the gunman has already won. He did everything he set out to do. The children will lose only if we do not take the correct steps to protect them. Anything else would be stupid.

There is a sign on a restaurant that says "No Firearms Allowed". I won't eat there because the management is Stupid. If someone comes in and decides to shoot a few people one thing is guaranteed, no one will be there who will shoot back to stop him.

I heard one politician say that if everyone were allowed to carry guns it would end up in a "Dodge City Mentality" with shootouts a common occurrence. I assume that he was speaking of the old west Dodge City. The problem here is that you were safer walking the streets back in the old west Dodge City with a six gun strapped to your hip than you are in present day Chicago. Stupid is in here somewhere and it won't be hard to find.

I have one more thing to say about this gun debate. Each year hammers and clubs kill more people than rifles and to confuse the issue even more is the fact that nearly twice as many people are killed by hands and fists each year than by murderers who use rifles.

Banning assault rifles, which by the way you can't get anyway, won't fix this problem. We should ban hammers and clubs! Okay, what do we do about the hands? I know, everyone will be required to have handcuffs on when they leave the house. Boy this is really stupid. On top of that every year anywhere from 800,000 to 2.5 million criminal acts are stopped by private citizens with guns. Figure that one out Alma.

One more thing before I close this chapter, back in the old West there were not many horse thieves. That was because they used to hang them. You figure out what I mean by that.

Keep this in mind, protect and keep watch over your family because it appears that no one else will. And if you think all of this is just stupid, it's okay because after all, "Stupid is in the eye of the beholder".

Chapter 4
"Mom Got it Right"

Have you ever wondered where good manners have gone? Does anyone teach that stuff anymore? When I was a kid my mother taught me to say please and thank you and to be polite to my elders. Where has that idea gone? Now I think they give lessons in being rude because there are so many people who are really good at it.

My mother was generally right about most things. Not all the time though. She told us when we were kids that if we didn't rinse the soap out from under our arms we would get a fever. She was wrong about that. I know because I tried that in boot camp so I could go on sick call. I just got itchy armpits.

There are some lessons that you just don't figure out until you are older. Kind of like the itchy armpit thing. Other lessons are best understood when we are young before we let all the other adult stuff get in the way. Take pride for instance. Babies don't let pride get in the way when it's time to be fed. Adults allow pride to get in the way all the time. Someone offers help and pride jumps up and says, "I don't need any help!"

I'd like to tell you a little story about how I learned a lesson…

When I was in the Navy I didn't have much money. I didn't have a car and I never had enough cash for a bus ticket so I hitch-hiked. I hitch-hiked all over the place. I hitch hiked the five hundred miles from

Norfolk, Virginia to Groton, Connecticut just about every weekend I could get a 72 hour liberty.

On this one occasion I was stuck on the road coming out of New York City into Connecticut. I never liked standing on the side of the road. You never knew who would stop to pick you up. I use to go to gas stations and look around at the potential rides and ask the people who looked promising if they would give me a lift. That way I got to pick the people I asked. I looked for families and fellow members of the military and out of state plates.

On this particular day I wound up on the side of the road no where near a gas station. I had been standing there for quite a while when finally a guy stopped to offer me a ride. He didn't look too threatening so I climbed in. About five minutes into the ride I noticed that he had a gun under his shirt. That got me a little nervous.

Skillfully (I thought) I began working into the conversation that I was broke. It was true, I was broke I had a whole $2.50 on me. I was thinking that if he intended to rob me he would figure it was a waste of time. That was my usual strategy for robbery avoidance. I had used it on more than one occasion and since, up to that point, I hadn't been robbed I figured it worked.

I figured it worked again because he didn't stick me up and throw me out of his car. We talked about a bunch of unimportant things that I have long since forgotten. Eventually we reached the place where I was going to get out. He started to reach back to where he had the gun holstered and I thought here goes my $2.50. Instead of pulling out his gun he pulled out his wallet. He gave me every dollar that he had. He apologized for what he gave me because, in his words, "it wasn't much", but it was all he had on him. He went on to say that if he had more he would have gladly given it to me.

You see, he was a New York City cop on his way home from work. That explained the gun. He had a brother in the service and he knew what I was going through. He figured if he could help me he would be doing something good that day.

I don't know much about cops. I do know that they do something good just about every day. I also know that they don't make huge salaries. They risk their life everyday to keep the bad guys from taking the $2.50 we have stuffed in our pockets.

I know something else about that particular cop. There is a place in heaven marked out for him and the guys like him. That cop taught me about charity and about gratitude. He gave me a sense of gratitude that I will never forget.

There goes that hymn again sounding off in my head. "Have you done any good in the world today? Have you helped anyone in need?"

If by some really odd circumstance that cop reads this story I hope he will give me a call so that I can thank him for making me a better man than I was before I got into his car. My phone number is easy to find. It's on my website TageWright.blogspot.com.

I am a pretty friendly guy. I got that from my mom. That was how she was with people. I talk to everyone and so did she. I have a picture of her in my movie room. I think it was her High School picture. I can see why my dad fell in love with her.

She was only fifty seven when she died. It was only a few months from when the cancer was found until her passing.

I often think about the last time I saw her. She was up at Uncas on the Thames. She was not conscious and her breathing was labored. I stayed for just a short while and then went home to my wife and kids. I told my wife that I was sure my mother was going to die that night and she did. I wish that I had stayed with her and held her hand.

Her life was short but long enough for her to fall in love, get married and raise three children. She taught us well. She was a terrific mom.

When I enlisted in the Navy I was amazed and somewhat disappointed that she wasn't at all upset when I left home for boot camp. Long after her passing I learned from my father that she cried every night for two weeks over my leaving.

She wrote to me all of the time and I would usually find a few dollars tucked into those envelopes. Hey, where do you think I got that $2.50 I had in my pocket?

My mother was a great judge of character. I know that because she picked my dad to marry. She may not have been right about the soap thing but she got it right about everything else!

Chapter 5
"Common Sense"

I looked common sense up on Wikipedia and this is what I came up with;

Common sense is defined by Merriam Webster as, "sound and prudent judgment based on a simple perception of the situation or facts." Thus, "common sense" (in this view) equates to the knowledge and experience which most people already have, or which the person using the term believes that they do or should have. The Cambridge Dictionary defines it as, "the basic level of practical knowledge and judgment that we all need to help us live in a reasonable and safe way".

My dad called it horse sense. I like to call it not being stupid. After all, calling it common sense doesn't seem very accurate because it isn't all that common. In fact it seems to be downright scarce. Just look around.

Last week I went to the Navy Credit Union to cash a check. There is a sign on the window with a picture of a gun with one of those red circles around it with the red slash and the words "No firearms allowed on this property" printed underneath. I wonder whose idea that was? I'm sure that at least a dozen would-be bank robbers saw that sign and went to rob some other bank instead. You know, one that allowed them to bring their gun inside.

Here is another one for you. Did you know that the cost of making a penny is projected to surpass 2.41 cents for each penny made this year? In 2011, the US minted about 4.9 billion of the little rascals. The government could save about one hundred and nineteen million dollars by just not making any this year. Honest, just check it out for yourself at "Snoops.com". I think good old horse sense could fit in here somewhere.

On two occasions I served as a chaperone for my granddaughter's school trip to the Boston Museum of Science. While there, I sat and listened to a young fellow (the same guy on both occasions) talk about our putting 10% ethanol in our gasoline in an effort to save on the use of fossil based fuel and thereby making less pollution.

Really? Not so fast. Common sense really took a hike on this one. We are putting 10% ethanol in gasoline, which is less efficient (translation; lower miles per gallon so you burn more than with just straight gasoline) and creating that gallon of ethanol takes 1.3 gallons of fossil based fuel to complete the process. Basically, you have burned more fossil fuel trying to avoid burning fossil fuel than you would have if you hadn't tried to burn fossil based fuel in the first place. What the heck did I just say?

It just boils down to this; the individuals who came up with the idea in the first place lacked good old common sense and their good intentions were turned upside down by facts they basically ignored or didn't understand. There are a whole host of other problems that using corn-based ethanol has caused that I won't go into. None of them were good for our economy or us.

A fairly long time ago, someone with some common sense figured out that a whole bunch of gas was being burned while people waited for the stop light to change when all they wanted to do was turn right. As I said, someone with common sense had a great idea. So out came the new traffic law. You could now turn right after stopping at red lights unless otherwise posted.

Now comes the guy without common sense. Suddenly, at nearly every stoplight in the state, a new sign appeared. It read "no turn on red". Whoever had the contract for the signs made a few bucks on that one. After awhile most of the signs came down with a few exceptions. The guy with the common sense must have chased the one without it out of the office.

It's bad enough to be common senseless without purposely telling everyone about it as in the case of the good old bumper sticker. I love the one that reads, "War is not the answer". Those individuals evidently have never heard of the Civil War or the Revolutionary War or World War One or World War Two, or…. heck I could go on forever listing wars that were the only answer.

Don't get me wrong. I don't hold anything against anyone being commonsenseless (I think I accidentally created a new word). I get that way myself every once and awhile. And sometimes it can be down right amusing. Like the time my brother and I decided to build a dune buggy.

When my dad left for work that particular morning he walked right past my red, 1959 Volkswagon Karmann Ghia. Little did he know what would be there when he got home.

You may not be familiar with the Karmann Ghia. It used to be called the poor man's Porsche. It looked cool but definitely was short on horses in the engine department.

My brother and I were armed with some basic facts. We knew that to build a dune buggy you need some kind of Volkswagen. We had that covered. We had the Ghia. We also knew that a dune buggy had a shorter wheelbase (shorter distance from the front axle to the rear axle) than my Ghia. We had that covered too. We had a hacksaw. The one thing that we lacked was the common sense to realize that we had no idea how to put the two halves of the car back together again once we cut it in two. By the time my dad got home that evening my 1959 Ghia was in the garage in three pieces (we cut the top off because after all dune buggies are convertibles). He was not impressed.

On an interesting note later, while I was in the Navy, my dad built his own dune buggy from start to finish all by himself. He used the engine from my Ghia so it didn't go to waste. Not bad for a guy who only got to the eighth grade. He might have been short on formal education but he was long on horse sense and even at 90, he was one cool dad!

Unfortunately, there are too many times when people with power show a lack of common sense in what they do and it hurts someone else. I haven't been able to confirm this next story, but I have no doubt that it occurred. I heard about it a very long time ago.

Somewhere out west there is an area where wild fires are common. To protect the homes (rather expensive ones I might add) they made firebreaks. The firebreaks were made by disking the fields around the homes. This insured that the fires would not burn down the houses. It was extremely effective.

Along came a commonsenseless group of people who discovered there was an endangered critter in the fields around the homes. I believe it was some kind of mouse. You can guess what happened next. Disking was prohibited forthwith. After all, you might kill the endangered critter and then the owls that prowled the night sky would be denied their midnight snack.

The result would be obvious to someone who wasn't commonsenseless. The fires came along and burned down the houses. I might add that they roasted the endangered critter as well. Go figure.

So what do we do? How do we fix the epidemic (I love that word) of commonsenselessness? Hey, another new word! I'll have to contact Wikipedia and let them know. Maybe you have a few suggestions to correct the problem. If you do please share them with me! My email address is easy, TageWright@aol.com even I can remember it.

I went to bed last night thinking about what to do. The only thing I could come up with is how I learned whatever common sense I have. I didn't learn it in school. I learned it from my mother and father. Perhaps that is the solution, perhaps if we as fathers and mothers took the time to teach our kids some basic common sense they would, in turn, pass it on.

For this to work, we have to keep our families together because the biggest example of no common sense is what we have been doing to the family. I've said this before and I'll say it again, if you fail in the home, no other success will make up for it. The family is the key to a whole lot of issues. If you don't believe me do a little research. The facts are on my side.

Just one other thing we might do. The next time we see something that displays commonsenselessness we should say something. Even if it is just "that doesn't make any sense". Kind of like the home version of homeland security. Of course I really don't know exactly what homeland security actually does.

Hey, wait a minute. I just figured out how the government could save some big bucks this year. If they paid everyone who turned in their pennies a ten percent finder's fee on top of the cash value for each penny they turn in the flood of turned in pennies would make minting them this year unnecessary. I just know that there must be billions of the little fellas hiding out in piggy banks all across America!

For that paltry ten percent finder's fee they would save somewhere in the neighborhood of fifty million bucks! They could use that money to relocate those endangered mice. Just how much does it cost to move a mouse anyway? Nah, they wouldn't do that because nowhere in the United States is commonsenselessness more prevalent than in government.

Chapter 6
"Understanding"

It seems like a very simple word. Perhaps as a word it is simple, but as a principle it is anything but simple. It is in many cases the key to, well, just about everything from our relationships with others to our relationship with ourselves.

A long time ago when the eight track was the best sound you could get in a car I listened to the Moody Blues while cruising along in my 1965 Dodge Dart GT. There was one song, I don't remember the title, but in it was a line that went something like this, "Whenever I felt fear or knew pain I was not understanding". I think anger was in there somewhere as well, but since I can't locate the exact song I can't be sure. That line made a forever impression on me.

We go through this thing we call life, listening (well sometimes) looking around, and talking. How often do we really understand what our senses take in? And just as importantly, how well do those we have contact with understand what we really mean when we do all that talking?

Movie tips:

In the movie "P.S. I Love You" there is a line that really struck a chord with me. In a scene in the beginning of the movie the soon to be deceased husband is arguing with his soon to be widowed wife. He asks her if they are arguing about what he said or what she thinks he said.

When I heard that I wanted to jump up and shout "Yes" because I suddenly had an epiphany (whatever that is). I am convinced that most people especially husbands and wives spend a good part of their time arguing about what they think the other person means without really knowing ... well, you get the idea.

Just what is it you want?

In thinking about all of this I was reminded of the story I once heard about a Mom whose young son Jimmy came running in from playing with his friend down the street and asked, "Where did I come from?"

The Mom knew this day would come so she had planned way ahead. She prided herself on how well she planned ahead for life's little hurdles. Even though this was much sooner than she had expected she was ready. She sat the boy down at the kitchen table and began to explain all about the birds and the bees and how little Jimmy had managed to show up at their house.

She thought it went very well. Little Jimmy sat there listening to his mother without even asking one question. It took seventeen minutes. It must have been the short version. I got the long version from my mother, it took almost an hour and to make matters worse, my older sister was listening in. I don't remember if she actually said anything but, well, it's one of those things that can't forget.

When she was all done she smiled at her son and asked him if he had any questions. He said yes, just one. He was wondering where he came from because his friend Tom down the street said that he was from New Jersey.

Just who is your audience?

The one person in the world who needs to understand what you mean when you speak is your spouse. They should be number one on your list. They are your most important audience. If they are not number one, then your priorities are in need of repair. In some cases a complete overhaul might be in order.

Just consider this, remember those signs right before the construction site that read, "Fines Doubled"? Well, when your spouse misunderstands you those fines are tripled. They are not strangers who you can just walk away from. You are tied to them with a bond that is more important than any other attachment you have with anyone else.

Be forewarned, you may find yourself explaining your explanation of your explanation of what you really meant when you first said what it was you said that they didn't understand in the first place. Confused yet? Just wait it gets better!

I didn't say that this would be easy. In fact it can be downright challenging and that is the easy part. It not only takes two to tango, it takes two to foster good understanding. You have to work together. You give this a thought; you can't expect to be understood if you refuse to make the effort to understand your spouse or anyone else for that matter.

You two have an advantage!!

You do have an advantage with your spouse you don't have with anyone else. You can both sit down together and make the commitment to work on better understanding (some people call this communication). Caution, if you try this with a coworker there might be a problem.

Set some ground rules!

You might want to set some ground rules to help you along. These would be things that neither one of you would violate. It might be good to write them down. With my memory it would certainly be a good idea. Where was I? Oh yeah, ground rules:

1. Be honest, don't lie about what you meant when you said what it was you said. After all if you didn't want it understood you shouldn't have said it in the first place. It would also be a good idea for you to know what you meant. It makes explaining it much easier.
2. Avoid getting angry. Anger is a weakness not a strength. It spreads like fire and destroys any chance of being understood.
3. No shouting! Honestly, the loudest voice does not win you anything. Unless you are entered in a cow calling competition.

4.   Stay on track. When you start to head off in the wrong direction you need to get back on track.
5.   Pay attention! That means don't try to listen to your spouse do anything else at the same time. I think they call it "undivided attention".

You don't need to use these particular rules, they are only suggestions. You can make up your own. Your situation is different from everyone else's. If you can improve the understanding between yourself and your spouse you are on the way to a happier life.

I believe that the "understanding" part is more important than the communication part. After all communication is useless if the person you are communicating with has no idea what you mean.

As for all of the others that you are in contact with, learn how to say what you mean and as they say, mean what you say. Did you ever wonder just who "they" are? All I know is they sure say a lot.

Your ears are made for hearing but it is your brain that was made for listening. Just try to have them both in gear at the same time and everything will work out just fine.

Trying to understand and be understood is something that takes commitment. If commitment isn't something that you are big on, sort of like if you are living together not wanting the commitment of marriage, well just ignore everything I just said about spouses. You will probably be heading off in different directions in the end anyway.

One of my friends who was living with a woman had a way of putting it. He said, "why should I buy the cow when I can get my milk for free. Do you gals understand what he meant by that? It's just something to think about.

A side note for all of the guys out there. The saying "happy wife, happy life" is not just a saying. It is a secret formula for success in many cases.

One last thought, try not to assume you know what someone means when there is even the slightest doubt. Just remember, the captain of the Titanic assumed it was safe to take the course he did. We all know how that turned out.

You know, it never hurts to say to your spouse, "I don't understand what you mean". I wish I had the presence of mind to say that when I'm not getting it.

I think that is all I have to offer on this topic. Remember to keep a smile on your face and twinkle in your eye. I have no idea where you can get the twinkle.

Chapter 7
"Imagination"

It's midnight; do you know where your imagination is?

I am nearly sixty-eight years old. That means that I get a senior discount in a whole bunch of places and sometimes I get the buy one get one free at the casino buffet on Mondays. It also means that I can remember a childhood where imagination was what you needed to have fun. What happened to that wonderful concept? Where did it go?

I remember sitting in my bedroom reading a book. Besides you, who does that today? There are still a few, I suppose, but I am sure it is a very few. After all, reading takes imagination. You see the story in your head. There are no actors, no special effects, only you, the words in the book and your imagination, a daunting task for some of the youth of today not to mention a whole bunch of adults.

Yes, I remember sitting there with a reading lamp being the only light turned on in my bedroom. Can you even buy a reading lamp anymore? Would they know what you were asking for if you did try to buy one?

Well, anyway, I was reading the book "When Worlds Collide". Philip Wylie and Edwin Balmer wrote it in 1933. It was a great science fiction story about the world coming to an end. You can probably still find it in the library. Check it out.

My imagination was in overdrive on that one. I recall quite vividly thinking that getting my homework done didn't matter much because the world was about to come an end. Then I remembered that it was just a story. I was torn between the joy of realizing the world wasn't about to end and the sad realization that I had to finish my homework. I hated homework.

Imagination was in the driver's seat for just about everyone back then. Today there is a distinct lack of imagination required for most of us. I'm beginning to think that the advent of the color TV might have been the start of the decline. It went downhill from the point where you could tell the color of Hoss Cartwright's vest. It was brown by the way. If you already knew the color of his vest or who he was for that matter, you are as old as I am, or you have Netflix.

Back then, the love scenes were a fade out and you imagined what happened next. Not now, no imagination is required. I'm sorry, but I don't think that was an improvement. It has also made it impossible for some of us to watch most PG-13 movies with our teenage grandchildren. If you know the guys or gals that came up with what a thirteen year old is supposed to watch send me his or her address. I want to give him or her or both for that matter a piece of my mind.

Take movies today, there may be a shortage of imagination in that department as well. If it isn't a remake of an old movie, it's a film version of a comic book. I think I am becoming cynical, and I don't even know what that word means.

I write fiction because it's my imagination that keeps me going, and besides, real life is too scary. I have always had a problem reading about real life brutality. It's the same with movies. I have never been able to watch "Schindler's List". I started to once and I stopped a short way into the film, my apologies to the people who produced it.

Without imagination there would be no airplanes or cars or a whole bunch of things that make our lives better. We need to foster it in our children and in my case, grandchildren. I'm not saying that we should ban all those things that leave out or stifle our imagination. However we do need to limit them.

I have told my readers before that I play video games on line. I have a PS-3 and at present play a game called Call of Duty Black Ops II. It doesn't require much imagination to play the game. It's ironic that some of the things like this video game that requires no imagination to play required a great deal of imagination to create. I guess there was some kind of trade off in there somewhere.

Do you want to create imagination in your kids? Read to them when they are small. If they are older locate some games you can play as a family that require imagination to play and I am not talking about video games.

Have dinner as a family and tell stories while you are enjoying the food. Don't be afraid to talk with your mouth full (although I would caution against laughing with a mouth full of mashed potatoes).

Life is full of adventure when you have the imagination to see it. You are never too young or too old to start on the path to a better and more fulfilling imagination. You can start today by picking up a book (preferably fiction) and start on page one. By chapter two you will be off and running.

I've got an idea, you can purchase a copy of my novel "Operation Armageddon" and ... Sorry I couldn't resist putting in the plug for one of my novels.

Anyway, start today and help build a better and more imaginative tomorrow. As they say on "The Five" on the Fox News , just one more thing, remember to let your family know that you love them every day and don't forget to feed the dog. If you don't have a dog, feed the neighbor's dog.

Chapter 8
Planning Ahead

Don't life's trials just seem to sneak up on you sometimes? If we could see into the future it would make planning ahead so much easier. When my brother was a little guy he was pretty good at planning ahead.

I remember this one time when he committed a spanking offence. That was back when you could get a spanking without the cops coming in with a SWAT team to take your dad away to jail. I don't remember what he did but he knew well in advance that he was going to get it. He planned ahead.

Our father came in and put him over his knee and gave him the spanking. Charlie cried and generally made a good show of it. My father put him back on his feet and left the room.   As soon as he was out of ear shot my brother wiped away the crocodile tears and started to laugh. I was confused to say the least.

My father always said that giving us a spanking hurt him more than it did us. In this case he was literally correct. My brother had really planned ahead this time. He had put some comic books in his pants to shield his butt. It worked like a charm.

To this day I can't explain my father not knowing the comic books were there. I suspect that he went into the living room and told my mother about Chuck and his armored butt. They both probably laughed even harder than my brother did.

If we only knew when it was time to stuff the comic books in our pants a lot of life's difficulties could

be avoided or maybe softened just a little.
Unfortunately that isn't the way it is a most of the time.
Most of the time, they occur without much warning.

Quite a while back my wife began filling empty
bottles with water and storing them all over the place. I
complained more than once about the water filled
bottles. They took up space. They got in the way of the
stuff I wanted to store. Besides I couldn't picture
myself drinking water from any of them. Who knew
how long the bottle was sitting there building up unseen
critters that would turn into something nasty inside of
me. That couldn't be good for you.

But like my own mother, the mother of our
children, my wife is generally right about a lot of things.
She was right about the water. When a hurricane came
through and the power went out we had water for
something I hadn't thought of. We had water to flush
the toilets. So if there were some unseen critters in
those bottles they have now been processed by our
septic system.

We eventually got a generator so we can pump
water even when the power is out. But guess what, we
still have the water bottles hanging around the house
and I am not going to complain. I wouldn't want to be
wrong two times in a row about the same thing.

That reminds me about something else I better
stop complaining about. There is a bunch of stuff in the
trunk of our car that I have been complaining about.
It's some food and, get this, water bottles filled with,
well, water. There is some of our old clothes and some
other stuff I hesitate to describe in there as well. It's

called a 72 hour kit. My wife put it together. It's for us if we have to go on the lamb. I complained because it takes up space in the trunk. I figured you should put it in the garage. Hey, the trunk is needed for other things like golf clubs and such. Of course I don't play golf, but I might take it up someday.

The other day a house in town burned down. I listened to the news report and was glad to hear that the family got out safely. That's when I figured something out. If that happened to us I guess the food and stuff in the garage wouldn't' be of much use. My wife was right again.

So even if life sneaks up on you there are some things you can prepare for. Keep some water around even if it is only to flush the toilet. Have a 72 hour kit stuffed in the trunk of your car. Keep some cash aside you can grab if you have to run for the hills.

Before I close this time I'd like to say a little about my dad who had just turned 90 when I wrote this chapter. He has always been a great father when we were growing up and even at 90 years old he was still a great dad. He lived in Florida and I called him every day and never hung up without telling him I loved him. For you men out there who might just take the time to read this book, start planning ahead so that when you son or daughter talks about you when you're ninety they will say, "he is a great dad".

Remember this you guys out there, nothing you do out there in the world will count if you have failed as a father and a husband. For the two of you, husband

and wife if you want your spouse and your children to love you, you need to love them first.

The best preparation advice I can give you is to love each other. Contrary to what Ryan O'Neal said in "Love Story" love doesn't mean never having to say you're sorry. Love is knowing when to say you're sorry.

So remember, keep the comic books stuffed in your pants, the water bottles in the trunk and I almost forgot, keep a smile on your face. After all, it's the most attractive thing you can put on and it doesn't cost a thing.

Chapter 9
Measure Twice Cut Once

Measure twice, cut once. Have you ever heard that expression? It applies to a whole lot more than cutting a piece of wood. It is a behavior that can be applied to most of the things you do in your life. I'll give you a personal example. In one of my blogs I quoted the cost of minting a penny. The blog was titled "Common Sense" and is also a chapter in this book. I only measured once and then I cut the board. That was a big mistake.

One of my friends, who read my blogs, sent me an email telling me that he used his common sense and checked out my figures on the web site I provided the link for. Guess what he discovered, I had made an error. A penny will cost 2.41 cents to make this year not $2.41 as I put forward in my blog. Boy was I way off. Speed-reading just doesn't do it some of the time. Fortunately I corrected the error for this book.

I had contemplated sending him a response telling him that it was a test to see just who would bother to check my facts. Or I could tell him that I am planning on using it on my application to apply for a job at MSNBC. I heard that they don't check their facts very well either. Either way it was an error. I apologize for the error which reminded me that anyone can make a mistake. There is an upside even to mistakes.

The bright side is I have friends looking out for me. Hey! If MSNBC isn't hiring maybe I could get a job in the government. They also don't seem to care about the facts of just about anything and you can make one mistake after another and still keep your job!! In fact you might get a promotion!

If those two don't work out I could become a weather forecaster. Everyone knows they get it wrong on a regular basis.

Back to measure twice. It's really a simple thing to do. You make your measurement and check it once more before you cut the wood. In theory you can catch your errors before you ruin the piece of wood. The only real problem is that most people will make the same mistake more than once.

And then there are other things you need to look out for. There is the one-inch error. That is when you get the fraction on the wrong side of the inch mark. That results in your piece being exactly one inch short. The simple fact is that sometimes we see something that isn't what we are really seeing. Confused? Trust me it gets better.

I spent about thirty years running a home improvement business part time. It was my second job. I discovered I liked doing that kind of work back when I built my house. Up until then the only thing I had ever nailed together was a little cabinet that was used to hold my Atari game system. Anybody remember those things?

I read a book somewhere that said if people knew how easy it was to build a house all of the contractors would be out of business. Yeah, right. It wasn't easy but it was fun. It was "on the job" training.

I had an old fellow helping me with the framing. Actually, he was showing me how to do it. His name was Rubin Mason. He was in his seventies and had a wealth of knowledge to draw from. I can still see him walking backwards on top of the 2X4 wall like some kind of circus performer. We were putting up the roofing trusses. On my best day I couldn't do that.

If anyone knew the rule about measuring twice it was Rubin Mason. In fact he didn't even like using two different tape measures on the job. He insisted that they produced different results. He might have been right about that.

One of his boys was working with him. He was about fifteen at the time. His name was (and still is) Will Mason. As young as he was back then he knew all about measuring twice and cutting once.

As I said in the beginning of this piece, measuring twice and cutting once is something that applies to many aspects of our lives. Measuring the things we are about to do twice before we do them could save us some heartache.

Talking about measuring, here is another one for you that you might have heard. It is to "Take the measure of a man". It means a lot more than the size of his suit. It's something all you gals should try to do before you say yes to that first date, and frankly if he doesn't measure up both times (measure twice girls) do the cutting thing. It is much easier sooner rather than later. For those girls just reaching the age when the dating thing comes along I have a three word warning. **Don't trust boys!**

There are an awful lot of people that will tell you not to judge others. You know, judge not lest you be judged. I'm here to tell you that if you want a life relatively free of avoidable problems you had better learn to "take the measure" of those you associate with. That, in a word, is "judgment".

There is a difference in judging others in the biblical sense and judging others in order to avoid some real pitfalls in life. My mother used to tell me that if I hung around with the wrong crowd I'd get in trouble, that's where measuring twice came in. Believe me, she was right about that.

There are many things in life that just happen without warning and are simply unavoidable. However, there are a larger number of things that happen to us because of decisions we have made.

Those are the places we need to measure twice. We need to do our research and make the right choices. There are pitfalls in making judgments about the people around us. We need to look out for those. On that particular note there is an interesting video about judging others you might be interested in watching. It is called "Looking through Windows" you can find it on YouTube. It is put out by Mormon Church. It is worth watching. Almost half of a million people have watched it already. Perhaps some of them figured out the point and added it to their lives.

I know a young woman who spent some time taking the measure of someone she thought she was going to marry. She had been going with this young man for many years before she actually thought about how he measured up to what she wanted in a husband. It was a very hard thing to do but she saw that there were important things missing in the relationship so she walked away.

It wasn't because he was a bad person or that his nose was crooked or his feet to big. I believe it was because the path that she wanted her life to travel went in a different direction than his.

When she finally discovered the man who she felt "measured up" it set the course of her life on a path together with her new husband. After several years of marriage and a few kids later she says with complete honesty that there is nothing about her husband she doesn't like. She chose wisely.

I would agree because I know the guy personally and I have never met a better man. The really neat thing about that is my wonderful wife totally agrees with me! I love it when that happens.

How many of us can say the same? If you are still breathing it isn't too late to learn how to measure twice before you cut the path for the rest of your life.

So here is what we do. We choose wisely. How do we do that? That part is more difficult. If I were an expert it would be easy for me to answer that question. But you see at nearly sixty-seven I am still learning. I do know this however, we need to surround ourselves with the things that lift us up, not those things (or people for that matter) that bring us down.

Be choosy in who you pick for your friends. Take their measure at least twice before you decide on whom they will be. Develop a set of basic core values and stand by them.

If you are looking for a spouse look in the right places. When I was in the Navy I spent a lot of time in bars all around the world. I know from experience that quality marriage material does not regularly populate those places. And besides they all thought my name was Joe.

Here is the hardest thing of all; you must always try to do the right thing. Just knowing what is right is not enough. You have to choose the right and do it.

We all make mistakes. It is part of being human. The mistakes we will regret the most will be those that we know we caused by making wrong choices. The regret is even greater if we knew at the time we made the choice it was the wrong one.

Measure twice my friend and cut just once. You will save more than a piece of wood.

Chapter 10
"What's in Your Orange"

About twenty-five or thirty years ago a good friend, Nellie Vernott, gave me a couple of tapes from a guy by the name of Wayne Dyer. He was someone I had never heard of before she gave me the tapes. You should look him up and listen to some of the things he has to say. Like fine wine he has gotten better with age. Not that I would really know much about the wine deal since I gave up wine a very long time ago.

Anyway, that was a long time ago and I don't really remember much from those tapes, except for this one thing that has stuck with me for all these years. What was in my orange? I've used this story on more than one occasion because the point Doctor Dyer made can help us understand an awful lot about ourselves. It sort of went like this…

If you pick up an orange and squeeze it what happens? The answer to this question is obvious to anyone who likes fresh squeezed orange juice. Out comes orange juice. That was easy. It's the next question that had me wondering if Doctor Dyer had all of his ducks in a row.

"Why?"

I thought, well, gee, that's because it's an orange and that is what's in it. How dumb a question was that? If this was a motivational talk I was missing the point. It sounded more like an advertisement for Tropicana orange juice. I love that stuff.

While you are figuring that one out, here are a couple of other things that I've noticed. There seems to be an epidemic of bad behavior in the world today. It's like pollen in the spring; it's everywhere! I'm not sure but I think that it has something to do with that orange.

I play video games on line. It's my son in laws fault. He gave me a PS3 several years back. I mostly play the war games. Call of Duty Black Ops is one of them. In this game you and your teammates play against another team.

I play hardcore. I have a three to one kill ratio in that game (no brag, just fact). That means I die once for every three of the enemy that I knock off. Not bad for a 66 year old gamer.

In that game mode you can kill your own teammates either by accident, or if you are a jerk, on purpose. There are an awful lot of jerks out there. I'm pretty sure that this has something to do with that orange as well.

People are stealing the pipes out of houses to sell them for scrap. They are stealing ornaments from graveyards and selling them for scrap too. Once when I stopped at the Seven Eleven near the Mohegan Sun Casino someone stole a toolbox from my truck. If that wasn't bad enough they stole my lunch box too! I liked that lunch box. I think that there was an orange in it.

A little while ago the Secret Service guys were kicked out of some country for arguing with a hooker over her fee. Some other gal was on the news because she thought someone other than herself should pay for the contraceptives for her recreational sex while she attended college. What was that about?

I remember what my mother had to say about girls who had recreational sex. It wasn't very complimentary. This also most certainly involves that orange. I think you will see what I mean in a minute or two, honest.

If you think about it, oranges are really useful. They provide vitamin C and other good things like fiber (when you get over sixty that somehow becomes important) and on top of all that they taste good too. I just peeled one a little while ago and ate it.

While I was taking the peel off I remembered something from back when I was in the Navy. With a little effort you can fix it so that when you squeeze the orange something else comes out other than just the orange juice. You can fix it so that a screwdriver comes out. No kidding!

You might know where I am going with this. All you need is a really large hypodermic needle, a shot of vodka and the orange. You inject the vodka into the orange and shizzam, you have a screw driver (vodka and orange juice) disguised as a harmless orange. Eat a half a dozen of those and you will need a designated driver to get home.

So, by now we have figured out that what comes out of the orange may not be just orange juice. You see, if you put something else in there, when it gets squeezed something else will come out. We are all kind of like that orange. We may look like an orange on the outside but what have we been putting in our orange? What have we been putting inside ourselves?

What kind of music do we listen to? What kind of movies do we watch? What kind of company do we keep? Do we have a moral compass at work inside of us? Do we even know what that is? Do we have character? Do we have integrity? Are we the same person when no one is watching us?

Just this evening Fred, a friend of mine, said that he teaches his children that character is doing the right thing even when no one is watching. He is putting something good inside the two little oranges that he is raising. How about you?

Almost anyone is a good enough actor to put up a good appearance for those people around them, but very few of us are good enough actors to maintain that orange like exterior when the pressures of life squeeze us. Whenever that happens, whatever we have been stuffing in our orange comes squirting out. It usually makes a pretty good mess when it does.

I'm convinced that those guys or gals killing their teammates in that call of duty game have got something in their orange that shouldn't be there. After all, the old saying "it's not whether you win or lose that counts, it's how you play the game" is a statement on character. If you figure that most of those people playing are young adults and kids, I'm starting to wonder just who has been filling their oranges?

So what do we do? What do we do if for years and years we have been injecting our own orange with stuff we know shouldn't be in there. Do we just say that's the way I am too bad for the other guy? It's like the bumper sticker I saw yesterday that read, "my attitude, your problem".

The confusing part was that right next to it was one that read "mean people suck". I'm not sure that I want to know that person. It was bad enough that I had to chase that car through three stoplights to read both of those bumper stickers. That wasn't easy in the 1984 Ford F-150 pickup truck I was driving.

Several years ago another friend of mine, George, was giving a talk at church. He said something that at the time I thought was pretty stupid. He said, "If nothing changes, nothing changes". Well, I was the one that was stupid because he was exactly right. If you don't make some kind of a change nothing will change.

There is a basic law of physics at work here. Two objects cannot occupy the same space at the same time. What we need to do is put enough orange juice back in our orange to force the other stuff out. If we work at it we can empty all the bad behavior from our orange. It may not be easy or it may not happen quickly, but you can do it.

Pay attention to what you are surrounding yourself with. If you listen to music, listen to good up lifting music. If you use foul language, stop using it. Many years ago I was working on a car with a friend of mine, he banged his knuckles and yelled out "rutabaga". He then told me that he was trying to stop his cussing. It worked for him.

The problem for most of us is identifying our own bad behavior. Once we do that we can change it. Knowing what to change is the key.

I remember the story I heard about a supervisor who had a lot of bad stuff in his orange. He worked at a plant that I myself worked at for nearly twenty years. He had some kind of a seizure. He couldn't speak or move but he could hear. When he collapsed one of the two people with him asked, "What should we do?" the other guy answered, "Let the SOB die".

Allowing for the guy who said "let the SOB die" having his own issues, the supervisor suddenly realized that the people who worked for him actually hated him. It could have gone either way but in his case that revelation changed his life for the better. He fixed his orange.

If you are still alive you can fix your orange. Then when someone asks you what's in your orange you can proudly say, "Orange Juice".

And if you have a bag of little oranges running around your house you can get right to work filling them with good things. One piece of advice, keep away from the vodka.

Remember to kiss your kids and tell your spouse that you love them and when you bang your hand remember to yell rutabaga.

Chapter 11
"Are You a Fault Finder?"

Are you the kind of person that can spot a fault in something or someone from a mile away in a blizzard? There are plenty of people who think this ability is an attribute. We can't be fooled by a smile or a kind word. No sir, we know what is behind that pretend niceness! We know what you are really thinking.

While I was thinking about this I was reminded of a story I once heard about a young man who had found the perfect woman to take to wife. I don't remember the story exactly as it was told or who told it so I will retell it in my fashion with apologies to the originator for any deviation from the original.

A young man had the occasion to meet a beautiful young woman who he fell in love with at first glance. She was beautiful beyond his wildest dreams. Her hair, her eyes even the shape of her face brought a quickened beat to his heart.

Shortly thereafter he asked for her hand in marriage. When she accepted his heart was filled with joy. One week to the day later they were married in the little chapel down the lane.

When she raised her veil standing at the altar for their first kiss as man and wife the young man saw something he hadn't noticed before. There on her right cheek was a small birthmark in the shape of a heart. It was so tiny it had gone without notice until just that moment.

The Little Things by Tage Wright

As time passed with each morning sunrise the young man would gaze at his wife lying there sleeping beside him. He would look at her face and think what an angel he married. She was perfect except for that one little mark.

The days turned into weeks and weeks into months and then it happened. One morning as he gazed upon his wife's face he noticed the mark had doubled in size. Then with each successive morning it continued to grow. Then on one morning he awoke to find it covered her entire right cheek. It was the most hideous thing he had ever seen.

This was more than he could stand so quietly he packed his meager belongings and left leaving only a short note. It read; I can no longer stand to look upon your face.

When his young wife awoke she found the note and after reading it she sat in front of her mirror crying. She looked at her reflection in the mirror and wondered what had happened to make her husband feel that way. She wondered what had changed.

She wiped away her tears and tried to get ready to face the day. She put a small dab of makeup on the tiny birthmark on her right cheek and she again wondered what had changed.

How many times in your life did a fault you saw in someone or something become the focus of all of your attention? How often has a tiny fault, like the young bride's birthmark, grown to enormous proportion while you watched? It is a real easy trap to fall into. People everywhere do it all the time. How about you?

There is another factor at work here that you may not be aware of. I once was told that police officers involved in a high speed chases begin to have tunnel vision. They become so focused on the car they are chasing and lose track of everything else around them. The results can be tragic. You may see the connection here. When we become so focused on someone's faults we not only lose track of what good that person has in them we just might also miss the good in others as well. We become the victim of our own form of "tunnel vision".

When it comes to fault finding most of us are nearsighted or maybe farsighted I can never quite figure out which is which! Well, I looked it up and farsighted is what I mean. We can be pretty good in finding faults in others but we somehow don't catch sight of the ones that we have, the biggest of which might just be the fault finding itself.

There are several people in our lives where finding fault can become a real problem. One would be your employer. If you find fault enough times with that guy or gal you might be looking for a new job. Getting hit in the pocket book usually gets our attention. There are still others that I will get to later that can have a much greater effect on our lives should we go fault finding with them.

Don't get me wrong, there are times when finding fault can be a good thing! Pilots check their planes for faults before they take off. That kind of fault finding saves lives. Introspective fault finding can be effective in helping you improve as a human being and I am guessing that would be a good thing too. Of course in this case we need to be sure that what we are looking at within ourselves is really a fault!

I know some people who think being kind is a fault. The same goes for generosity or believing in God. There are a whole host of things that some people might think are faults which actually are virtues. I guess that is where it gets confusing.

I'm sure you have had the term "constructive criticism" thrown at you at one time or another. The same guy who thought that one up told everyone that the Hindenburg was the future of aviation. I ask you, do you know anyone who really likes a critic? I know for sure that I don't.

I have a friend who told me that he always says no when his wife asked him to do things around the house. I was surprised because I always try to do what my wife asks me to do. I thought that was just what a husband did.

He informed me that when he does do things around the house his wife will criticize how he did whatever it was he did forever but if he just says "No" the complaint time was way shorter. That sort of makes sense, I think.

I don't think that his plan worked very well. They are no longer married to each other. Perhaps on the next go around they will both learn how to treat their new spouse.

On the helping out around the house deal, I had another friend who told me he got out of doing the dishes by doing a really lousy job at it. His wife got to the point that she wouldn't let him near the sink if there were dishes in it. I guess he didn't mind the criticism as long as he got out of doing the dishes. Hey, I guess that could be called constructive criticism!

You have probably guessed by now that I believe the one place where fault finding really doesn't belong is in a marriage. On top of that I wish t I could say I have the answer to exactly how you accomplish that little deal. I haven't figured out exactly how to eliminate it completely myself so I can't say I am an expert. But then, being an expert doesn't make you right. Consider this little tale.

There was a young wife who heard from some expert that she should have an honest talk with her husband. She should let him know about the things about him that she didn't like and he could do the same. Then, according to the expert, they could make changes so they could improve their relationship. I think the expert called it "good communication".

So that was what she did. She made a list of all the little things he did that annoyed her. It was just a bunch of little things that bugged her. She sat down with her husband and went through the list. He sat there and listened. When she was all through she asked him what it was about her would he like to see changed.

He replied, "nothing, you are just perfect the way you are". It took a long time for her to stop feeling bad about what she had done to her husband. She suddenly realized that all of those little things that bugged her weren't very important after all and the expert's advice in this case was not so expert.

The Little Things by Tage Wright

The real trouble with finding fault is that we can be wrong as many times as we are right. So exactly what do we do if we are a fault finder?

I guess it is sort of like when we are overweight. We stop eating so much (stop finding fault) and do some exercise. Anyone who is overweight knows how easy that advice is to follow. It is the same with fault finding with the exception that you can't look in the mirror and tell if you are a fault finder.

Here is a news flash, even if you aren't a fault finder you may find more happiness in your marriage if you just practice some anti fault finding techniques just in case. Here are just a few, you may think of even more.

1. Don't criticize your spouse for those little unimportant things that just bug you. And if the big things won't kill you ignore them too!!

2. Look for something good each day that your spouse does and tell them about it. It will not only make them feel good it will build your own appreciation of them as well.

3. Never part company without telling your spouse you love them and a kiss would be great.

4. Don't hang up the phone without telling them you love them.

5. Do one good thing every day for your spouse. Even if it's just taking out the trash.

Five is enough for now, but I'm sure that you have gotten the idea. Just on a side note, one time I was in the store in line to check out. My wife called to ask me something or other and when we were done talking I said "Love you" and hung up the phone. The woman behind me said "Gee, that was so sweet. I wish my husband did that". Maybe he is reading this book.

I know two guys who from my perspective have learned how to not be a fault finder. One's name is Eric and the other one is Joe. I would like to tell you a little about the two of them.

Eric is a soft spoken fellow about my age. When I asked him what he thought was a way of not finding fault he told me a story. It was about a couple who were on vacation.

They arrived at the hotel overlooking the water. When they entered the room in which they were going to stay the husband looked at the wall of windows and the ocean beyond. The breeze was blowing the curtains and the view was spectacular. To the husband it looked like something out of a movie. As he put the bags down he was carrying he heard his wife say "We aren't staying here".

The first thing that came to his mind was that his wife was going to ruin their vacation. But instead of saying the first thing he thought of he did something he had trained himself to do instead. He asked his wife one simple question in a loving manner. "What's wrong?"

She told him what it was she saw when she came into the room. There was a big stain on the carpet, the place was filthy and the previous guests had left some things behind.

Eric then told me that everyone comes at life from a different perspective and one way not to find fault is not to jump to a conclusions. You need to try to understand what it is they see that you don't.

Now it's Joe's turn. I've known Joe for a very long time. I have seen him in action with his wife and his kids. I have never seen him get angry. I have never heard him raise his voice. His wife tells me that he doesn't get angry. All in all if he has ever found fault in anyone he has kept it to himself and that is a good thing.

If I didn't know better I would think he was on some sort of medication that most of us could use. If he could bottle it he would make a fortune.

So what can we take away from Joe? I think it starts with self control and ends with a happier life. I also know that if Joe's children grow up to be like their dad the world will be a much better place.

So to all of us fault finders out there, when we find a fault in someone we need to look for an attribute to cancel it out and remember to keep our mouths shut until we find something nice to say! Bite your tongue if need be. I might need stitches before my training period is over!

And remember this, you and your fault finding will never change the person in whom you are finding fault. The end result will be how they see you and you may not like the faults they see in you.

So just keep smiling (it confuses the fault finders and scares the pants off of the mean ones) and if you want to find fault, learn how to fly an airplane.

Chapter 12
"Spending Time"

What do you do with your time? Have you ever really thought about how you spend your time? Most of us have to work to survive, although there are a growing number of people who make a career out of living off of the public dole. In more cases than you would think it isn't out of necessity it is a career choice.

Anyone who works for a living knows that time has a dollar value. The kind of work you do often determines the amount that someone will pay for your time. That is just the way it is. If you fly airplanes for a living you make more than if you wash dishes. It makes perfect sense to anyone with a firm grip on reality that some skills are worth more than others.

Here is where it gets a bit confusing. The value of your time is not the same as what someone will pay you for your time. In the long run you and only you will determine the value of your time. How much your time is worth is determined by a whole bunch of other factors as well.

When you play a video game like one of the Call of Duty games the time you spend playing the game is logged. You can go back and see just how much time you have spent playing the game. I have often thought about how much time I spend playing those games. I play six different characters. For just Call of Duty Black Ops Two I have logged over 566 hours. That represents over three and a half months of work at a full time forty hours a week job. That is in a word, crazy! I think that I may need to attend video games anonymous if there is such a thing. See what happens when there is no mom to tell you to stop playing those video games!

Now that we know I don't always spend my time wisely, how about you? Do you spend your time in useful pursuits or do you do what I have done with my allotted time?

I was relating the game thing to a young man at church and instead of commenting on my wasting my time he asked a question, "Did you have fun?" That got me thinking because even though I answered yes there was something in me that was saying no at the same time. I was a bit confused by that.

Many years ago I gave a talk at my church in which I spoke about how I had come to view money. Basically I said that to me money no longer was measured in dollars and cents, but rather in the hours of my life. If I were to purchase something I would look at it as giving up hours of my life for the item. When you look at money in that respect the things you spend it on take on a completely different look.

The time we have here on this earth has a number. Very few of us know what that number is. It's like a bank account, only we have no idea exactly how much or how little we have in it. Each day we make our withdrawal and each day we make our purchases. Most of the time we don't even think about the account we are drawing from until we get old enough to figure that there isn't a whole lot left.

The question for all of us is not simply what have we purchased with the minutes of our lives but when it is all said and done what has been the value of those minutes.

I have a friend named John who keeps a book in which he writes down every cent he spends and what he spent it on. He does this so he can look in the book and tell if he has been wasting his money. It also helps him figure out how to save money.

Imagine if you did the same sort of thing with how you spent your time. Imagine if you kept a journal of everything you did for one week. A record of how much time you spent on each endeavor right there for you to review. You might be surprised at what you would see.

When it comes right down to it, how we spend our time is an indicator of what we think is valuable. What do you think is valuable? What in your life do you think is worth spending the minutes and hours of your life doing?

It seems to be a human condition that those things that are the most valuable to us are not compensated for in cash. When you stop on the side of the road to help a stranded motorist or take care of an elderly parent your time is worth more than can be calculated in dollars and cents.

I spent some time a few days ago watching two of my grandsons. Now that was time well spent. It was worth more to me than any of the roofs I shingled or the instruments I calibrated.

As I look around I wonder just what is happening to us as a people. We seem to be losing focus on what is really important and what is really of value. Consider this, when I was a kid the most important thing to my mom and dad was our family. Where is that line of thinking today? Check out just a few statistics, 48% of births are to unwed mothers, forty to fifty percent of first time marriages end in divorce. Exactly where are we headed? Exactly what do we now think is of value? We use to have family values. Where have they gone?

You can't make anyone else spend their time wisely or make right choices. You can only spend your own time wisely and make your own choices the right ones. Perhaps the next time you are about to do something that you think up front is a waste of time or the wrong thing to do you will reconsider what it is you are doing.

Just one other thought before I leave this chapter. In 1995 there was a local Playwright's festival at the Eugene O'Neill theater center. One of the plays performed there was one that I had written titled "A Rare Encounter".

It was a story about a man named John who had lost sight of the value of his own life to the point of wanting to end it. That is until he meets Charlie an old bum who knew a lot about wrong choices.

With wisdom learned the hard way Charlie teaches John a lesson or two. I later turned the play into a short novel titled "Spit Shine". It is a story you might enjoy and if it doesn't make you laugh you should check your pulse because you might be dead.

In great measure most of us learn about wrong choices by making them. On rare occasions we learn from other people's mistakes. I say rare because we generally have the "it won't happen to me" idea that gets in our way.

One thing I know for sure, wrong choices do waste the minutes of our lives. Once they are gone you never can get them back.

I had a friend once named Bill who would get about four opinions from different people before he did almost anything. I thought he was nuts. Now I know why he did that and well, he wasn't nuts.

I'd like to add one last thing about the play "A Rare Encounter". When the performance was done and the lights came up there were several people in the audience who literally had tears in their eyes. I was overjoyed to learn that those tears weren't because the play was so bad, it was because it had touched them in a special way. I knew then that my time writing the play had been well spent.

Chapter 13
"Turtle Envy"

I think I am suffering from turtle envy. Perhaps there are or were as the case may be times in your life you have had the same affliction. Before I get into the particulars of this not so rare condition, I would like to say a few things about our hard-shelled four-footed friends.

He may move slowly but as that rascally rabbit can attest, he always wins the race. On top of everything else he brings along his own little fort that he can retreat into at will.

They may look like rocks with arms and legs but they can swim like a fish, well sort of. And there isn't just one version. There are many different kinds, and some of them live a really long time.

There was an Indian Ocean Giant Tortoise that was captured as an adult. They figured he (I guess it was a he) was about fifty years old. I have no idea how they could figure that out. Anyway he/she/it lived another one hundred and fifty two years in captivity. Now that's a senior citizen.

They have been plodding along at their slow but steady pace for about 200 million years. Did you ever wonder how they figure that stuff out? Heck, I have trouble figuring out the expiration date on a can of soup. I want to meet the guy who figured out when the first turtle showed up. He could probably answer the age old question, "what came first, the turtle or the egg".

Where was I? Oh yeah, turtle envy...

The Little Things by Tage Wright

Wouldn't it be nice if when life attacks you from all sides you could just pull your arms and legs and head inside a nice hard shell and wait it out? Yeah, that would be great.

I envy the turtle. There must have been some point in time when the critters trying to eat those turtles were successful. I know that because God made a couple of modifications to the design. He came up with the Box Turtle. I really envy that one. He not only can hide in his shell he has a front door and a back door that he shuts behind himself.

I guess if you think about it lots of people act like turtles. They may not have a hard shell to crawl into but they find other ways to "hide out". Booze is one way lots of folks hide out. If you drink enough you forget your troubles for a while. Not a very long while, but for a little while. The trouble with that "hide out" is that when you climb back out the situation has probably gotten worse on account of the booze.

Physical pain is another reason we might want to hide out. As far as I can tell the only physical pain that brings us joy is the pain of childbirth. Not that I know much about that. Even so lots of moms would like to find a less painful way to bring a brand new person into the world.

Back when our first child was born, before they let the dads into the room while the new arrival was showing up, I sat in the father's room waiting. I could hear my wife and knew by the sound of it she wasn't having much fun. I wasn't the one in pain but hearing

71

the woman you love in pain makes you want to hide out until it is all over.

Emotional pain can be even worse than physical pain. With physical pain you may be able to pull back into your shell by "taking a pill" and away goes the pain. I remember when I had surgery (twice) and they had me hooked up to some kind of deal where all I needed to do when I was in pain was to push a button and in went a shot of morphine and bingo the pain magically went away.

Human beings are very adept at figuring out ways to avoid the things that hurt them. That is if they plan that far ahead. A good part of the time we can't avoid troubles or pain. That's when we envy the turtle the most. Only there is a problem because the turtle only seems to be able to hide out and that might not solve the problem. I know this from firsthand experience.

One day I was driving along and I saw a turtle all tucked away in his shell. He was in the road about four feet from the side of the road. The passing cars had frightened him so he was doing what came natural to him, he was hiding in his shell.

I had seen this before a long time ago. A turtle's shell might be pretty strong but it's not strong enough to support the weight of a car. He, at least at the time I thought it was a he, wasn't aware of how much danger he was in sitting there in the road.

I turned around and parked my car in the traffic lane and got out. I picked up the little guy and put him on the side of the road that he headed for. I was really happy it worked out because the last time I tried the same thing the results were a disaster. I'll explain that a bit later.

I called my dad on my cell phone while I was completing the rescue. So the news of my heroic effort was reported to my 90 year old dad 1400 miles away in Florida. That's when I learned the turtle was probably a girl. He told me that this was the time of year that they crawled out and dug holes to lay their eggs.

How many times in your life have you been half way to your destination when something has forced you back into your shell making you immobile? How many times have you been sidetracked or stopped completely by circumstances or events (or people) that you didn't anticipate?

It was at that moment I had a revelation. I realized something I should have figured out a very long time ago, but hadn't. I realized my envy for that hard shelled reptile was sadly misplaced.

Hear me out, don't envy the turtle. His best defense is to hide within his shell. If the rabbit only knew that little fact he would have always won the race. All he needed to do was scare the turtle and the race would have been won.

On top of all that no shell for the turtle or for us that is strong enough to provide complete protection. The things or people in this world that want to crush us, or our dreams, won't be fooled by our hiding out in our self made shell. To make things worse, we make an easy target when we sit there all curled up inside of ourselves.

I'm not going to envy the turtle any longer. No, not me, I'm going to envy my neighbor's cat instead. Why? I'll tell you why. We had a really big black Labrador named Betty (she weighed in at about 100 pounds) and she really liked to chase cats. Well, most cats anyway.

I watched her one day when she attempted to chase my neighbor's cat. She started barking and charged at the cat ready for a fun chase. What happened next surprised both me and Betty. That cat turned hissed and ran at Betty. The sight of a one hundred pound black lab being chased by a cat the size of the dog's head was just too much. I think I laughed for about a week.

Yeah, I'm getting a case of neighbor's cat envy. The next time troubles come looking for me I'm going to turn the tables on whatever it is. You need to do the same. When life attacks you attack back.

Remember the old saying about when life gives you lemons you are supposed to make lemonade? The heck with that! When life gives me lemons I'm going to pick them up and toss them back where they came from and then I'll go find me some oranges!

I almost forgot, about that first turtle that I tried to save. I pulled over to the side of the road figuring I'd get out and help him across the road. Well, the car behind me pulled around me and ran smack over that turtle. That's when I should have realized turtle envy is not where it's at.

Chapter 14
"Who's Looking out for the Kids?"

Just who's looking out for the kids? I think that is a fair and important question. The answer should concern all of us because as it has been said by the infamous "they", "the children are indeed the future".

One thing that I have always known about kids is that they are much more fun than grownups. By their very nature they just want to have fun. When they laugh, they really laugh and when they cry, you know there is something wrong. After all they haven't yet learned how to hide how they feel about things and the art of lying believably has not yet been developed. I wonder just where they learn how to do that?

I think I get along so well with kids because they think I am one of them and they are right. At nearly sixty seven I might be the oldest kid in my neighborhood or the town for that matter and I feel good about that.

I was an assistant cub master for the Cub Scout pack at our church for a couple of years and before that I taught primary at my church. Primary is the class for the kids. The one thing that I have always been certain of is that if you have a job involving kids you have a responsibility no one working with adults has and it is the truth.

I have noticed the tendency of people now-a-days to shirk their responsibilities. That's not what my mother taught me!! It may just be that you know what I am talking about or you more than likely wonder what it has to do with kids.

I looked up the word shirk. I just wanted to be sure it meant what I thought it did. Whenever I do that I discover things I didn't know like "shirk" is an intransitive verb or it can be a transitive verb, whatever they are! I probably shouldn't have slept through English class. Of course I slept through history class too but I got an A in that one. Perhaps even "sleep learning" can be selective!

Getting back to the kids, kids ask questions. I read somewhere that preschool kids ask their parents about one hundred questions a day. When we grow into teenagers the question asking has slowed to a trickle and in some cases it stops altogether. That is with the exception of the "Can I borrow the car?" question that shows up around their 16th birthday.

I am sure that one of the biggest reasons they ask so many questions is curiosity. They want to learn. They want to figure out the world around them. They are building who they will be when the questions go down to that trickle I mentioned. That is why if you have something to do with kids you better be on your toes because they are always watching you and even before they can put together a sentence they have the question thing going on.

With all of the crazy things going on in the world the question just "who is looking out for the kids?" has become more important than ever. The problem is that there are a lot of people who claim to be looking out for the kids who really aren't. It may be intentional or just stupidity it's hard sometimes to tell the difference and sometimes there isn't a difference. I have no respect for those people.

What I would like to do here is tell you about three people who I know with certainty are looking out for the kids. One is a Teacher, one is a Doctor and third is a special type of Performer. Each of these three individuals are really special people with a special responsibility that they do not "Shirk".

The Teacher;

His name is Mark. He teaches at an elementary school. Even though I have known Mark for many years there were things I didn't know. When I asked him why he decided to become a teacher I discovered that he is a fourth generation school teacher.

Mark really likes kids and I know that they really like him. I once saw a note written by one of his students when he was leaving one school to eventually work at another. Kids don't write notes to bad teachers or ones they don't like.

When he sees a kid he sees the potential that the child has hidden inside where someone else might not bother to look. Maybe you remember a teacher or two like Mark who made a lasting impression on you. I know without a doubt that he is making impressions on your kids if they are fortunate enough to be in his class.

Each morning when Mark gets dressed to go to work he doesn't figure that he is going to go out and change the world. Perhaps once in a while he might dream of doing it but he knows like any good teacher that the impact on the world which he will have is measured by how he helps those in his charge to eventually face the world and make the right decisions.

That is an awesome responsibility, but teachers like Mark are up for it. Mark told me that when he walks into that classroom "It's on" and from that point the words he uses, his body language and even his facial expressions need to be all directed to help the kids learn not only the lesson being taught but the lesson about what kind of person they want to be. Anger whether expressed in word or deed has no place in that room.

While I talked to Mark about his job I discovered something else. Mark was brought up by great parents. It reminds me of my own feelings about my parents. It also reminds me that the greatest teachers of all should be our parents. Sadly though, today that is not as true as it was when I was a kid.

In fact the percentage of children born out of wedlock is staggering. Before I started looking into it I never would have guessed that 40.8% of births in the US are to unmarried women. As far as I can see those kids have a disadvantage right out of the starting gate. I might start an argument there but then I care about the kids not the PC police.

One last thing about Mark, although I am not technically a kid he has taught me a lesson or two as well. One time when I was working on something in his bathroom his son who is the same age as my granddaughter came to me with a can of soda. He asked me if I could open it for him. I said "sure" and did just that.

A few minutes later I overheard Mark ask his son where he got the soda. Then he asked the question that taught me a lesson. "Who opened it for you?" His boy, being taught successfully to tell the truth said, "Tage". That's when I learned that sugar before bed for a kid may not be good. I also heard in his voice the love and patience he has for his children. We should all be as fortunate to have a dad like Mark.

The Doctor:

His name is Fred Santoro but the kids just call him "Doctor Fred". Doctor Fred is a pediatrician. I've seen Dr. Fred work close up. I've watched him with my grandchildren. You can tell a lot about a person by watching and listening if you take the time to do that. If you can't tell that Doctor Fred cares about the kids he takes care of you can't tell white from green.

There are very few people in this world who actually figure out what they want to be before they get out of High School. There are even fewer who actually become what they want to be. They are a special breed. That's Doctor Fred.

While still in High School he wanted to be a pediatrician. Even though while in medical school he saw many different medical specialties he still zeroed in on pediatrics. Was it money or the quest for fame that was his inspiration? Not a chance.

Doctor Fred had something growing up that we all really need. He had two "very loving" parents. There were also four other kids running around the house with little Fred sharing those loving parents. In that home was laid the foundation which would someday become Doctor Fred. I'm sensing a pattern here, how about you?

Doctor Fred said he enjoys watching the little ones in his care develop into young adults. I suspect there is something else going on here as well. I suspect that he has an inborn desire to make a difference in the children's lives that goes way beyond the medical side of the equation.

He remembers what it was like to be a kid. He remembers what he feared about going to the doctor. He also remembers what he enjoyed about those visits to the doctor. He hasn't simply filed those memories away. He uses them to relate to the kids and their parents. It works!

I know it works because my grandchildren look forward to their visits with Doctor Fred. They know he is there to help them and I know that my daughter trusts Doctor Fred. My daughter is a very good judge of character.

One point Doctor Fred made to me was that the children's welfare is dependent on adults and it follows that pediatricians have a great responsibility to look out for them and their families.

Parents and children put a lot of trust in their pediatricians. For a guy like Doctor Fred that means that he puts the kid's needs ahead of his own. In his words, "It is a sacred trust".

Doctor Fred takes joy from watching the kids grow and develop into self sufficient adults. There is a reward here that goes beyond that money or fame thing. It goes to the core of what makes us human. It is the fulfillment of being able to help kids and their families during times of illness or stress. In his words, "It is great to make a positive difference".

What is the downside? Well Doctor Fred doesn't much like the paperwork or the time needed to get authorization for appropriate medications or the tests needed for the kids. That is where his passion starts to feel like a job, but it is worth it. Just ask him.

The last thing I would like to say here is that if you need to put your trust in someone to be looking out for the kids, Doctor Fred is a safe bet!

The Performer:

His name is Steve Elci. I had a look at his website. That is when I learned a couple of more things I didn't know. The first thing I discovered was that Steve writes the songs and music he and his friends perform.

Looking at the picture on his website I realized something else. I discovered that one of his "Friends" is the daughter of a couple that we have been friends with for many years!

I wanted to know why he chose helping kids as a career. I loved his answer. He told me that he chose helping kids after the birth of his children. His love for his own children inspires him to write songs that will have a positive impact on the kids who listen to them. I am thinking that Steve is also a great and loving parent. I am definitely sensing a pattern here!

It gets even better. He has a test for the music that he writes. He asks himself if it is a song he would want his kids to hear and that isn't all there is to it. He also wants the songs he writes to help the world in which the kids live. To use his words, "It's a career in helping kids and families through music. It's what I am meant to do".

I also wanted to know what kind of impact he was trying to have on the kids. You might think he already answered that question and in a way he partially did. Only the goal you have may not always match the reason you started something. Again, Steve doesn't let the kids down.

Steve's goal is to use a medium that has been successful for thousands of years in inspiring people. Music and song! He has a goal when he gets going on a song. He wants the lyrics and the melodies to be catchy enough to make the kids and the parents sing and listen to the song over and over again so that the positive message in the song sinks in. I would stress the word positive! Any good teacher or parent knows that repetition is a great way to teach a child. Sometimes even the grownups can get the message. And in Steve's own words "positive messages can reach far and wide".

The last question I had for Steve was if he felt a special responsibility dealing with kids. Here is what he said.

"The talent that was given to me (writing children's songs) I take very seriously. I feel it is my responsibility to use this talent to better our children and future through music. This talent was designed for children but not limited to them as I make conscious decisions to design my songs for parents to enjoy as well. Families singing my music and enjoying time together inspires me to write more songs. It's a wonderful feeling."

I have no doubt that Steve and his friends are looking out for the kids!!

If you take anything away from this I hope it is that looking out for the kids is something that we all should do. Kids need good loving parents. They need a safe place to grow into adults. They need good examples in the adults they encounter. Does anyone today even know what that means? Are you looking out for the kids? I hope so!

Remember the pattern we saw in all of this? Good and loving parents. If you take it upon yourself to have a child, whether you are the mother or the father, it is your sacred duty to be the best parent you can be.

I'll leave this chapter with this final note, love your kids and watch over them, they are the greatest treasure you will ever have.

Chapter 15
"Respect"

I've been sitting here trying to figure out what to write about next. I thought I might write about the ten suggestions. They were formally known as the Ten Commandments, before the politically correct and the "I don't believe in God" crowds got wind of them. Then I remembered my visit to my dermatologist. There in the room where I waited for my examination was a notice that gave me the topic I'd like to write about. Later I will explain about that notice.

I was brought up in a home where we were taught respect. I am not sure if very many homes have that particular objective high on the list of things to teach their kids. There certainly isn't much respect displayed over all in the public sector.

What is respect? Aretha Franklin had her own definition of respect which she put to song. Boy that gal can sing!

I looked respect up on-line and the definition had me more confused than I was before I looked it up. I had to get half way down the page before I realized I was looking for the verb form not the noun deal. That might explain my problem with English in High School.

I thought I actually knew the definition of respect before I looked it up. Then I discovered that I didn't know the half of it (whatever that means). A while back we had a cook out with the cub scouts. Before we headed out to try and start the next great wildfire (we couldn't let New Mexico out do us) we had our opening exercises. We do the pledge of allegiance, the scout promise and then an opening prayer.

The boys rushed through the pledge of allegiance with everyone saying it at a different speed. It was not acceptable. I stopped them at that point. I told them what I am about to tell you. I spent four years in the Navy and seven years as a buck Sergeant in the Army National Guard. I put my life on the line to defend the flag and all that it stands for. It deserves respect. When we (any of us) as Americans say the pledge we should say it with respect.

When I was a young man in my twenties I was tough. I could and did on a few occasions stand toe to toe in a ring and trade punches with someone else foolish enough to do the same thing. I could hit a four-inch bull's eye with an M-16 at one hundred yards and do the same thing at fifteen yards with my four inch 38 special.

I may have had all that tough guy stuff going for me but every time they played the Star Spangled Banner or Anchors Away tears would come to my eyes. I had learned respect for my country, the flag and the freedom we have here in this wonderful country of ours. It is a freedom that was paid for by guys like me who wore the uniform of the United States Armed Forces.

Respect covers a lot of ground. It has a lot to do with how you treat those around you. It isn't possible to show respect and be rude at the same time is it?

I realized something yesterday when I was talking about this with my teenage granddaughter. She said something that really makes a lot of sense.

Basically she said that if you are nice to people first it heads off their being rude to you. Sort of like a pre-emptive "show respect for others" strike.

I started to think about the fact that most people I come in contact with are nice. Then I thought about what my granddaughter said and wondered how many of them didn't get the chance to be rude because of my pre-emptive smile. I draw it like a gun.

The way we behave in public shows everyone around us how much respect we have inside of us. Take the characters that use profanity in public places. I am a firm believer that in some cases profanity is a crutch for people with a limited vocabulary. In other cases it is a direct result of having no respect for those within earshot.

Have I ever used profanity? Hey, does a bear defecate in the woods? I jumped around that one didn't I. I was a sailor and a soldier I know a bunch of nasty words you probably haven't even heard. Even back then when I was a sailor I had enough respect for others to not use profanity in mixed company or in front of people I didn't know very well.

I remember back when my ship, the USS Belknap, was in the shipyard in Virginia a yard worker remarked that he had noticed I didn't cuss like my shipmates. He meant it as a compliment so I didn't have the heart to tell him it was because I didn't know him.

Lack of respect seems to be running deep these days. It's not gone for good, respect that is, it's just on an extended vacation. At least that is what I am hoping for. Our day-to-day lives can be improved by just a little respect.

At the start of this I mentioned a visit to my dermatologist. Her name is Annette Headley and she is a great doctor. When I showed up thirty minutes late for my appointment (I had the incorrect time) she accommodated my error. Her staff is polite and very nice to talk with.

While I was awaiting her examination I noticed a printed notice on the wall in the examining room. It basically stated that some patients have exhibited rude and sometimes abusive behavior towards the staff and noted that if you did that you would be asked to leave and would not be welcomed back. I can't imagine what would make someone behave that way in her office. My conclusion was simply it must be a lack of respect laced with liberal amounts of ignorance.

Respect starts with each of us as individuals. It's called "Self Respect". I'm sure you have heard of it. Once you have learned how to respect yourself you can move on to the other forms of respect. I find it difficult to imagine someone who can't respect themselves, respecting someone else.

The rules are pretty simple. To be able to respect yourself you need to emulate those things that generate respect. Would you respect someone who tells a lie at the drop of a hat? That would be number nine on the list of ten suggestions. If for you the answer to that question is no then you might have trouble having self respect if you lie out of hand yourself.

Here is a list of three things that you can do to build your own self-respect;

1. Be honest, that is don't lie.
2. Don't take things that don't belong to you (don't steal things)
3. Don't cheat on your spouse (adultery).

You know what this is starting to sound like the list of those ten suggestions! Go figure!!

I guess in the long run it's like the golden rule with a small modification. You just need to respect others the way that you would want to be respected. It isn't all that hard to do. And you don't have to know them to respect them.

Start today for a more respectful tomorrow. After all, respect is like that saying "what goes around comes around". Just put it out there and it will eventually come right back at you.

You might want to review those ten suggestions I talked about earlier. They worked for Moses perhaps they will work for you. You know who Moses was, don't you? He was the guy that parted the Red Sea. He had all that white hair and looked a lot like Charlton Heston.

Chapter 16
"Honesty"

Honesty, is it just another lost virtue? I have been wondering about that lately. Just turn on the news, someone always seems to be lying about something. It might just be the new national pastime.

There are a lot of virtues that have been left by the side of the road. The one I thought of when I was working on the chapter about "Fault Finding" was honesty. As you look around you how many truly honest people do you really know? Is it just me or is there a distinct lack of honesty in the world today?

If you are a politician you don't really lie you simply misspeak. I just love that one. I remember the controversy over Richard Blumenthal's supposed misspeaking about his military career and who could forget Bill Clinton misspeaking about Monica until that blue dress showed up. In the last presidential campaign Senator Harry Reid said on the floor of the Senate that Mitt Romney hadn't paid his taxes in ten years. It was a lie. It didn't matter to Senator Reid that he lied. It didn't matter that he undoubtedly knew it was a lie. It only mattered that it worked to discredit Mitt Romney. The objective was to cause Mitt Romney to lose the election and the truth was not important, only the goal.

I have begun to think that if Abraham Lincoln was alive today he just wouldn't fit in. He got the title "Honest Abe" for a reason. He was an honest man. You might want to check out more about honest Abe, it might just inspire you.

The Little Things by Tage Wright

The amazing thing about Abraham Lincoln was that he was a lawyer. Does anyone out there believe that many lawyers are honest? I know at least one lawyer who is honest. I'll get to him later. You might want to consider this observation. I was once told that a lie is anything true or false that is intended to deceive. Just spend a few minutes thinking about what lawyers actually do for a living. You might want to watch the movie "Liar Liar" with Jim Carrey.

Gone are the days when our heroes were good honest men and women. I'm not quite sure what happened to turn things so upside down. I turn on the radio and hear about athletes using drugs to gain the edge. I think that is called cheating. I play a video game on line and some of the other players are "boosting" to complete challenges. Basically, they are cheating too. They are cheating to win a reward. I just don't get it. If you can't complete the challenge honestly what kind of a reward is that?

There are, however times when a glimmer of hope arises to make me feel that I am wrong about this. A lady that I know drove off with her lap top computer on the roof of her car. It fell off somewhere in Norwich and she had no idea where. To her and my amazement someone picked it up and turned it into the police. She actually got it back! She had stumbled onto an honest person. That glimmer of hope was not bright enough to cancel her previous encounter with dishonesty.

That same lady had her car stolen (along with over one thousand dollars cash) only a short time before she lost the computer. Needless to say, she hasn't seen her car or the money since.

The problem for me is that I do not have a good enough memory to be an effective liar. It's that old line about the tangled web you weave when you begin to deceive. I'm sorry but I can't remember who I said what to. Basically, the truth is easier to remember and I actually forget that once in a while.

What I want to do here is talk to three special individuals and ask them three questions about honesty and pass along to you what they tell me. In the process perhaps my outlook on this matter will improve.

Here are my three simple questions:

1. How important is honesty in what you do?
2. Do you think that honesty is a lost virtue?
3. Many people are dishonest in order to get ahead financially or otherwise. Is that something that you think is justifiable?

The first person I would like to introduce you to is Lee Elci. Whenever I get up early enough I tune in to 94.9 FM and listen to his show from six to ten in the morning. You should try it because he is really worth listening to. He is certainly not just another pretty face. Come to think about it, that wouldn't matter anyway because he is a radio guy.

While Lee is on the radio the other Elci guy is taking care of the kids. I think there is another pattern developing here.

The Little Things by Tage Wright

How important is honesty to Lee Elci in what he does? On a scale of one to ten Lee feels honesty is a thirteen. You don't have to listen to his show for very long to get that impression. To quote him directly, "I can't think of a situation where a lie or misdirection serves anyone better than the truth. Personally and professionally, honesty is all I can ask from someone".

Honesty and character are important to Lee. "Say what you mean and mean what you say." That is something we have heard more than once. I'm beginning to think it is a basis for good character.

Is honesty a lost virtue? His answer made me think a bit and I am starting to lean in his direction. He said the following. "No... it's not a lost virtue, but I do find that there is an increasing number of people who have no issues with dishonesty."

I think that Lee is onto something and he has a solution for each of us to try. It is this, "the trick is to keep those people out of your inner circle".

Is being dishonest justifiable? Well for Lee Elci, honesty is not only the best policy, it is the only policy. "If it takes you lying or deceiving a friend or co-worker to better your situation it's a situation that is not worth having."

So the next time you tune into 94.9 News Now and you hear Lee Elci's voice you will know just what kind of man you are listening to. They are on line too so you can listen from anywhere in the world.

Earlier I mentioned one Lawyer who I know without a shadow of a doubt is an honest man. I have known this guy since he was a teenager. He is a lawyer, a journalist and a successful author. Here is what he said in response to my questions.

"Trust is the essential ingredient in what I do as a journalist. Without it I can't do my job."

He knows that honesty is one of the major building blocks of trust. But what about the lost virtue question? His answer put another chink in the armor of my first conclusion about honesty.

"Not really. There are still plenty of honest people. There are also those who are willing to discard honesty for personal gain. I just try to associate with people I can trust. Fortunately, the majority of my friends and colleagues are trustworthy people."

What about all those people that justify being dishonest to get ahead? I shared his answer with my wife. We both really liked this answer.

"No. But dishonesty is as old as the Bible. It's been around longer than The Ten Commandments. The best way to spread honesty is for parents to teach it to their children through example."

How about them apples? So, just who is this mystery guest? His name is Jeff Benedict. He is a journalist, an author, a lawyer and most important of all an example of honesty to his children.

My third and final individual I will call John. He is a retired corrections officer. This is one individual who has had close up contact with dishonesty. It was by his request that I not use his real name or identify where he worked.

I have known John personally for many years and I can vouch for his personal integrity. I was very pleased when he agreed to give me the answers to my questions. Although we talked on the phone his answers came in the form of an email.

John told me that as a corrections officer honesty is extremely important. I was surprised to discover the reason for that. This is what he said.

"Honesty builds trust between you and others. The reason why it is important, your word is everything inside of the correctional facility. If you are honest it makes your job easier and harder."

Okay, when I read that last sentence I thought he had made a mistake when he was typing it out, but then I read further and found it wasn't a mistake at all.

"Easier because, others learn to trust you and place confidence in what you do and say. Harder because, in the prison setting not all people are honest. Some expect you to lie for them to cover up their lack of control or immaturity. In other words they create problems and expect you to cover for them by lying. However, being honest is the only way to help others to be honest. I have found that by being honest, others respect you."

Respect, now there is a word I've heard somewhere before. It is funny how some things just run together isn't it.

When you think about it how much respect do you have for someone who proves to be dishonest? Can you trust them to be honest with you? Isn't being able to trust someone at the core of any relationship? In a marriage trust is one of the core building blocks.

When asked if honesty was a lost virtue he said something that I think most of us would agree on.

"If you take a look at today's politicians, then yes."

Do you think that most politicians are honest? If not, just what do we do about that? I've already pointed out a few examples of dishonesty swimming around in politics. There just might be a pattern there as well. I hope that I am wrong on that one but I suspect not.

He went on, "I have worked with a lot of people over the years. I have found that most are honest. There will always be a group that for one reason or another will be dishonest. I simply avoid people like that as much as I can."

There is a pattern I've picked up on here with these three. They all try to avoid being close to dishonest people.

John answered my final question about justifying dishonesty with this statement, "No, I don't think it is justifiable. Take a look at the papers and see what happens when people are dishonest in dealing with their fellow man. Prisons are full of people who are dishonest. To me at the end of the day, I need to look at myself in the mirror and know that I am right with God. If I'm not, then I need to correct my mistakes."

So what have I learned in all of this? For myself, I have discovered that honesty is not lost it has just been misplaced by a lot of high profile individuals. I've learned that honesty is an important part of many people's lives. I have also learned that no matter who you are, justifying dishonesty is in itself dishonest.

What do we do about this if we do look in the mirror and see a dishonest person looking back at us? How do we fix it? How do we straighten out the crooked road we have been traveling?

One of the unintended consequences of being a liar is that you think everyone else does the same thing. You end up in a place where whatever other people tell you become suspect. This is not good for you or anyone around you.

Here is the deal. It is difficult and sometimes impossible to straighten out the road behind you. You can however begin to walk in a straight line and believe it or not the people around you will sooner or later notice the change in your course.

If you have children show them what honesty is. As for those little white lies, avoid them because they add up! And you know those politicians that misspeak; well perhaps we should fire them until they figure out we are watching.

Just try this on for size, keep a smile on your face and truth in your words. As a wise man once said, say what you mean and mean what you say. I know that you have heard that one before. After all, repetition is a basic learning tool.

The Final Chapter
"A Hero Died on Sunday"

A hero died on Sunday. He died one month short of his ninety first birthday. I spoke to him on the phone for the last time on the Saturday before he passed away. He couldn't talk much or for very long because every time he said a few words he would have a fit of coughing. I told him about my day and what I was doing and when I hung up the phone I said what I always say to him and then we said good bye. I did not know that it would be for the last time.

He was certainly a hero. He wasn't a military hero. During WWII he couldn't get into the service because of a bad arm. He had been a breached birth and when he was pulled into this world it was by his arm and as a result his arm was damaged. It was always what he called his bad arm. He wasn't a famous sports hero or a famous actor. He never struck it rich or invented a better mousetrap. He didn't win the Indianapolis 500 or go into space. I guess that to most folks he was just Fred.

Fred had a scar on his right cheek. He got it from the handlebars of his bicycle when he was a kid. Like most scars it became less noticeable the older he got. You had to look really hard to see it but you didn't have to look very hard to see the character of the man behind that scar. You would, however, have to look long and hard for someone who didn't like Fred.

Fred was a little shy on the education side of things. He never went much further than elementary

97

school. Even so he had learned how to figure. While he was still a boy by today's standards his father charged him board to live at home. I remember him telling me that when he got a raise at the job he worked his father raised his board so the raise was gone. It wasn't long after that Fred took a room at a boarding house in town.

Fred worked a lot of places including doing some cooking at Seaside in Waterford, Connecticut. Back then it was for treating young people with tuberculosis.

While he worked there he met a patient named Sophie and they fell in love and were married. They had a daughter they named Jean.

When she was a little girl she was struck by a sled and suffered a ruptured spleen. She might have died except for the efforts of a surgeon named Tage Nielsen. He saved her life.

Fred couldn't pay Doctor Nielsen his fee because he didn't have the money so the good doctor told him to pay what he could when he could. So that was what Fred did. Then one day when Fred brought him a small payment Doctor Nielsen took the bill with a balance still owed on it and wrote across it, paid in full, and handed it back to Fred. Doctor Nielsen was a hero too.

I first met Fred on August seventh in 1948. From then until now he was and has been my hero. To everyone else he was just Fred, to me he was dad, and wouldn't you know he and my mother named me Tage Nielsen Wright. It is a name I am very proud to bear.

Everyone has a father, but not everyone has a dad, and not every dad is a hero. Mine was and is just that, a hero. He taught me more about life than any book I have ever read or any teacher I have ever known. He was a good, honest man who really said what he meant and meant what he said.

He taught me how to ride a bike and how to water ski. He taught me to be tough when I needed to be and how to put that toughness aside when need be. He taught me how to shoot a gun and how to take care of a family. He taught me to be honest and most of all he taught me what it meant to be a dad. He did all this and more.

Before he retired from Pfizer (I worked there as well) and moved to Florida I spent every day at lunch sitting with him in the paint shop having soup and talking. When he retired I missed those talks and when he moved to Florida I missed having him nearby.

For many years now I have called him every day and I would never hang up without telling my hero that I loved him. I will ask God each day when I say my prayers to tell Fred that we love him and miss him. There is a peace I have in this loss I feel because I know that now my hero is standing with my heroine Sophie watching over their children and grandchildren and great grandchildren.

I would like to take just a minute to thank someone else that I am certain in my father's eyes and mine as well has reached hero status. His name is Charles Frederic Wright and he was a surprise gift to Fred and Sophie two and a half years after I showed up. He, along with his wife Megan, labored taking care of our dad when neither myself nor our sister Jean could.

If you take anything away from this story, take this, anyone can father a child. It takes a man to be a dad and a special man to be a hero. If you are falling short in this take my advice and figure out how to be a hero. Or when you are gone the only one who will miss you will be the tax man.

It is my sincere hope that there is something within the pages of this book that will inspire or help you. That is what my father did and I hope I am half the man that he was.

After all is said and done it is "The Little Things" that can change our lives.

Author's Note:

If you have enjoyed reading this book I hope that you will recommend it to your friends. If you would like a signed copy for someone you may contact me at my email address (TageWright@aol.com) to purchase any of my books.

I appreciate the time you have spent reading this book. It is my hope that you have found something of use within its pages.

Other Titles by Tage Wright:

The Brotherhood of the Sword Trilogy

Operation Armageddon
Project Vengeance
Project Doppelganger

The short novel
Spit Shine

Made in the USA
Middletown, DE
30 September 2021

48662335R00060